DINOSAUR WORLDS
# FALL OF THE
# DINOSAURS

DON LESSEM

**Heinemann**

DINOSAUR WORLDS: FALL OF THE DINOSAURS
was produced by Bender Richardson White, Uxbridge, UK.

Editors: Lionel Bender, Andy Boyles
Designer: Ben White
Editorial Assistants: John Stidworthy, Madeleine Samuel
Media Conversion and Typesetting:
  Peter MacDonald and Diacritic
Production: Kim Richardson
Senior Scientific Consultant: Dr Peter Dodson, Professor of
Anatomy and Geology at the University of Pennsylvania
School of Veterinary Medicine, and Vice-President of the
Dinosaur Society.

First published in the USA in 1996 by
Highlights for Children, Honesdale, Pennsylvania 18431.

This edition published in Great Britain in 1996 by
Heinemann Children's Reference, an imprint
of Heinemann Educational Publishers, a division of Reed
Educational and Professional Publishing Limited,
Halley Court, Jordan Hill, Oxford OX2 8EJ.

MADRID ATHENS
FLORENCE PRAGUE WARSAW
PORTSMOUTH NH CHICAGO SAO PAULO MEXICO
SINGAPORE TOKYO MELBOURNE AUCKLAND
IBADAN GABORONE JOHANNESBURG KAMPALA NAIROBI

ISBN 0 431 05661 7 Hb   ISBN 0 431 05665 X Pb

British Library Cataloguing-in-Publication Data.
A catalogue record for this book is available
from the British Library.

Printed in Spain

**This book is recommended by the Dinosaur Society UK.**
**For more information please contact The Dinosaur Society UK,**
**P O Box 329, Canterbury, Kent, CT4 5GB**

**Acknowledgements**
**Photographs** Pages: 5: The Natural History Museum, London.
10: Ignacio Salas-Humara/Don Lessem. 15: George W. Frame.
16: Carlos Goldin/Science Photo Library. 20: Thomas
Jerzykiewicz/Don Lessem. 23: Dr J. A. L. Cooke/Oxford Scientific
Films. 24: George Holton/Photo Researchers/ Oxford Scientific
Films. 26: Don Lessem. 27(top): Don Lessem. 27(bottom): Don
Lessem. 30: Don Lessem. 34–35: Roger Tidman/ Natural History
Photo Agency. 37: Don Lessem. 40: Don Lessem. 44–45: Novosti
Press Agency/ Science Photo Library. 46 (top): Bruce Selyam/
Museum of the Rockies. 46 (bottom): American Museum of
Natural History. 47: The Natural History Museum, London.
**Illustrations** All major double-page scenes by Steve Kirk.
All other major illustrations by James Field. Ecology diagrams and
small featured creatures by Jim Robins. Step-by-step sequences
by John James. Maps by Ron Hayward.
Cover illustration by Steve Kirk.

# GLOSSARY

The Late Cretaceous Period lasted from 97 million to
65 million years ago. In the Late Cretaceous, vertebrates
included not only the dinosaurs featured in this book, but
also the following:

**Crocodilians** (krok-o-DILL-ee-uns) A large group of reptiles
that includes modern crocodiles and many extinct forms.
In the Late Cretaceous, some crocodilians were larger than
any meat-eating dinosaurs.

**Ichthyosaurs** (ICK-thee-o-saws) Fish-shaped, air-breathing
marine reptiles that ate fish. They lived throughout the
Cretaceous Period.

**Mammals** (MAM-uls) Animals with hair that nurse their
young. Mammals were present throughout the age of
dinosaurs, although during that time they never grew larger
than domestic cats.

**Primates** (PRI-mates) A group of mammals that includes
monkeys, apes and humans. The first primates appeared in
the Late Cretaceous. They were similar to squirrels in
shape and size.

**Pterodactyls** (TAIR-o-DACK-tills) Pterosaurs with long necks
and short tails that grew both small and large in the
Jurassic and Cretaceous Periods.

**Pterosaurs** (TAIR-o-SAWS) Flying reptiles, the first
backboned animals to fly.

**Reptiles** Animals that reproduce by laying hard-shelled or
leathery eggs on land. Snakes, lizards, turtles and
crocodiles are some of the modern types of reptiles.

**Sauropods** (SAW-ro-pods) Long-necked, lizard-hipped,
plant-eating dinosaurs that walked on all fours.

## ECOLOGICAL TERMS

**atmosphere** the layer of gases that surrounds the Earth;
also known as the air.

**badlands** any dry highland area with deep gullies caused by
sudden heavy rains. The Badlands of the western United
States is the best example.

**carnivore** a meat-eating animal.

**climate** the average weather conditions in a particular part
of the world.

**continent** a huge area of land on Earth, such as North
America, South America, Europe and Australia.

**environment** the total living conditions, including
landscape, climate, plants and animals.

**evolved** changed, over many generations, to produce a new
species, body feature or way of life.

**geography** the study of the land, sea and air on Earth.

**geology** the study of the materials of the Earth's rocks,
minerals and fossils and the processes by which they are
formed.

**habitat** the local area in which an animal or plant lives, for
example, a desert, forest or lake.

**herbivore** a plant-eating animal.

**migrate** to move from place to place as conditions change
or to reproduce.

**predator** a meat-eating animal that hunts and kills.

**prey** an animal that is hunted and eaten by a predator.

**scavenger** a meat-eating animal that does not kill its own
prey but eats the bodies of animals already dead.

**species** a group of living things in which individuals look
alike and can reproduce with one another.

**vegetation** plant life.

# ABOUT THIS BOOK

Welcome to *Dinosaur Worlds.* In these pages you will see dinosaurs as you have never seen them before – with their fellow animals and plants in the environments they inhabited. Dinosaurs were a highly successful and varied group of land reptiles with fully upright postures and S-curved necks that lived from 228 million to 65 million years ago.

*Fall of the Dinosaurs* explores the environments of the Late Cretaceous Period, which lasted from 97 to 65 million years ago. The majority of the dinosaurs we know thrived at this time. Then, perhaps suddenly, dinosaurs and many other animals on land became extinct. In the sea, many large creatures died out, too.

This book reveals these worlds as today's leading scientists and artists see them, based on fossil evidence. Fossils are the remains of once-living animals and plants that have been preserved in the rocks. Comparisons with living animals and habitats help to fill in details that fossils cannot provide.

*Fall of the Dinosaurs* is divided into four chapters, each looking at a specific dinosaur fossil site and revealing a different feature of dinosaur life and death. A short introductory section provides background information about the world at this time.

Enjoy your journey of discovery to the lost worlds of the dinosaurs!

"Dino" Don Lessem

**Measurements**
This book uses metric units of measure:
         centimetre (cm), metre (m),
         kilogram (kilo) and tonne
1cm = 0.4 inches, 1m = 40 inches = 3.3 feet
1 kilo = 2.2 pounds
1 tonne (1,000 kilos) is approximately 1 ton

# CONTENTS

Within each chapter of the book are five double-page spreads. The first spread is a large dramatic scene at the site millions of years ago. The second spread, 'A Look Back In Time', identifies and describes the major animals and plants in the scene and highlights the environment. The next spread, 'Featured Creatures', gives basic facts and figures about the most interesting animals and plants. Spread four, 'Then And Now', compares dinosaurs and their worlds with present-day animals and habitats. The last spread in each chapter, 'How Do We Know?', looks at the scientific evidence for all this – the fossils and what they reveal about the behaviour and ecology of dinosaurs.

# THE LATE CRETACEOUS

## CLIMATE

The last and most powerful dinosaurs appeared in the Late Cretaceous Period. We know these dinosaurs far better than those from any other time. More than half of all known dinosaurs come from the last 20 million years (85 million to 65 million years ago) of the dinosaur era. They include familiar favorites like *Tyrannosaurus rex*, the horned dinosaurs such as *Triceratops*, and the duck-billed dinosaurs. Recent finds are even more exciting, including the largest dinosaur of all and a meat-eater even longer than *Tyrannosaurus*!

Although temperatures rarely dipped below freezing, there was more seasonal variation in temperature and rainfall than earlier in the Mesozoic Era. The climate of the Late Cretaceous was more varied than in the earlier periods of dinosaur history.

### FOSSIL FINDS AROUND THE WORLD

This map shows the present-day continents and the dinosaur fossil sites from the Late Cretaceous Period. The four sites featured in this book are shown as red dots. **Argentina** was home to the largest animal of all time and to a meat-eater at least 13.5 metres long.

The Gobi Desert of **Mongolia** was nearly as dry 80 million years ago as it is now. But many dinosaurs lived there, including some meat-eaters that resembled birds, dome-headed plant-eaters and several kinds of small, intelligent predators.

### CONTINENTS

In the Late Cretaceous, the continents were taking their modern shape. India was moving north from Africa to its present position. North America and Asia were joined at a narrow northern connection during much of this period. South America and North America were still separated.

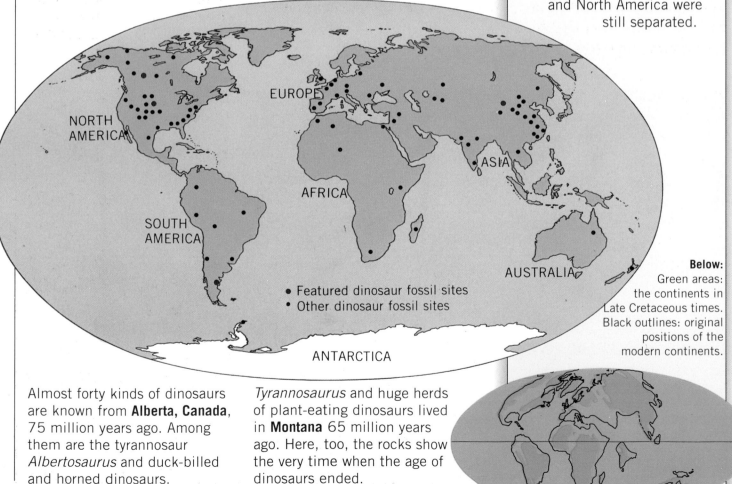

EUROPE

NORTH AMERICA

ASIA

AFRICA

SOUTH AMERICA

AUSTRALIA

- Featured dinosaur fossil sites
- Other dinosaur fossil sites

ANTARCTICA

**Below:** Green areas: the continents in Late Cretaceous times. Black outlines: original positions of the modern continents.

Almost forty kinds of dinosaurs are known from **Alberta, Canada**, 75 million years ago. Among them are the tyrannosaur *Albertosaurus* and duck-billed and horned dinosaurs.

*Tyrannosaurus* and huge herds of plant-eating dinosaurs lived in **Montana** 65 million years ago. Here, too, the rocks show the very time when the age of dinosaurs ended.

During the Late Cretaceous, sea levels were dropping again after reaching their highest point ever 100 million years ago. The environments of the Cretaceous continued to change. Conditions became far more like those we would recognize today. Grass had yet to evolve, but flowering plants grew in size and number until, by the end of the Cretaceous, they were the most common plants in some habitats. Dinosaurs were widespread, living in many climates – from the Arctic, where winters were cool, to the hot, dry lands of Central Asia. Mammals were still generally smaller than domestic cats. The first primates (squirrel-sized mammals that some scientists think were the ancestors of humans) scurried about in trees. The first bees and ants started to pollinate the flowers.

The dinosaurs that were the best-equipped for chewing plants, the duckbills, appeared. They were named for their spoon-shaped bills, which resemble those of today's duck-billed platypuses. In the Northern Hemisphere, the duckbills became the most common of all large dinosaurs. Armoured dinosaurs reached their largest size. So did meat-eaters. In the Southern Hemisphere, giant four-legged dinosaurs dominated the land, as they had done in the Northern Hemisphere millions of years earlier. Fossils show that birds became more common. Pterosaurs grew to record sizes, as big as fighter planes.

**Nests containing eggs of the Late Cretaceous dinosaur *Oviraptor*** (see page 23) have been found in the Gobi Desert in Mongolia. When first discovered, these eggs were thought to be those of *Protoceratops*. *Oviraptor* was named 'egg thief' because scientists thought it was preying on these eggs. New finds of *Oviraptor* embryos in the eggs, and four *Oviraptor* adults on top of the nest show that this dinosaur was the parent, not the predator, of these eggs.

# DINOSAUR ANATOMY: *T. rex*

Scientists and artists have the enormous task of trying to reconstruct prehistoric life. Here, *Tyrannosaurus rex* (*T. rex* for short) serves as an example of how different kinds of evidence are used to bring an extinct creature 'back to life'. *T. rex* was king of all predators in Late Cretaceous western North America.

## GEOLOGICAL TIME
Dinosaurs lived during the Mesozoic Era, from 245 million to 65 million years ago. The Late Cretaceous Period, 97 million to 65 million years ago, was the end of the Mesozoic.

## FOSSILS
Bones fossilize most often when sediment – sand and mud from rivers – covers the bone. Then minerals enter the bone, turning it to rock. Bones, eggs, dung, footprints and skin impressions can all become fossils.

## TAIL
*T. rex* held its long muscular tail high off the ground. The tail was strengthened by rod-like, bony tendons.

## SPINE
This is also known as the backbone and is made up of bones called vertebrae. An animal with a backbone is known as a vertebrate.

## SKIN
Scientists think *T. rex* had leathery skin with a pebbly texture. We have no idea of its skin colour.

## PYRAMID OF NUMBERS
The diagram shows the numbers of some typical land animals and plants that would have been present in the same habitat as one *Tyrannosaurus rex*. It is based on estimates by palaeontologists. Giant predators such as *T. rex* are at the top of a pyramid of thousands of organisms. Just below are smaller predatory dinosaurs and large plant-eating species such as *Triceratops*. The smallest creatures are at the bottom of the pyramid. To find enough food for its massive body, each *T. rex* probably had to roam over a large area.

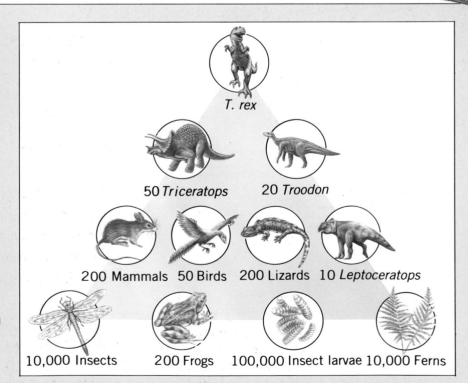

*T. rex*

50 *Triceratops*      20 *Troodon*

200 Mammals   50 Birds   200 Lizards   10 *Leptoceratops*

10,000 Insects      200 Frogs      100,000 Insect larvae   10,000 Ferns

Fossils do not hold the answers to every question about an animal's diet, posture, behaviour or internal organs. Only in the past decade have new discoveries allowed scientists to create a reasonably complete picture of the fearsome killer *T. rex*. Scientists can also reconstruct its life by comparing *T. rex* with living animals. In addition, some basic ideas about ecology – such as how many animals and plants might have lived in one habitat – hold true for many different kinds of environments.

*Tyrannosaurus rex,* or 'tyrant lizard king' was the last and largest of the tyrannosaurs. The only other big predator known to have shared its habitat was *Nanotyrannus*, a 4.5-metre-long, one-tonne 'pygmy' tyrannosaur. (See also pages 12 and 42.)

**SKELETON**
*T. rex*'s skeleton was a rigid framework that supported its body, protected its internal parts and provided attachment points for muscles used in movement.

**RIB CAGE**
The rib cage protected the heart and lungs, and helped the lungs expand and contract during breathing.

**NECK**
*T. rex*'s neck was short and curved. Strong muscles supported its head as it attacked and bit its prey (see page 47).

**SKULL**
The skull of *T. rex* was large and powerful. Inside, the brain was long and large for a dinosaur (see page 46).

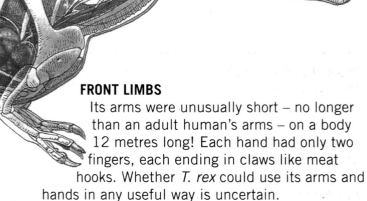

**FRONT LIMBS**
Its arms were unusually short – no longer than an adult human's arms – on a body 12 metres long! Each hand had only two fingers, each ending in claws like meat hooks. Whether *T. rex* could use its arms and hands in any useful way is uncertain.

**HIND LIMBS**
The upper and lower bones were long and slim, suggesting that *T. rex* could run fast.

**FEET**
Each foot measured nearly 1 metre across. The three large front toes had long claws. On the inside rear of each foot was a tiny toe.

## WAS *T. REX* THE BIGGEST HUNTER?
*T. rex* grew to at least 12 metres long and up to 7 tonnes in weight. But two newly discovered meat-eating dinosaurs – *Giganotosaurus* from Argentina and *Carcharodontosaurus* from Morocco – were bigger than *T. rex*. Individual allosaurs may have grown bigger than *T. rex*, and other meat-eaters, such as *Spinosaurus*, may have grown to the same size. But *T. rex* was the most fearsome predatory dinosaur.

# BIGGEST OF THE BIG
## PATAGONIA
### Argentina
90 million years ago

The footsteps of some of the largest dinosaurs ever to walk the Earth thud and echo in the South American forests. Huge plant-eaters browse high in the branches of the tall evergreens. They are alert, even as they feed, to the approach of a fierce predatory dinosaur, a meat-eater more than 13 metres long.

# WHERE GIANTS WALKED

The largest animals that ever walked the Earth are known only from fragments. Scientists suspect that these huge plant-eaters were herding animals, like elephants today. We do not know why these animals grew so enormous. Perhaps a lack of competition from other dinosaurs or the moist and warm climate may have helped these dinosaurs grow so big.

But by the end of the Mesozoic, the isolated dinosaurs of South America were far smaller and more peculiar. Some plant-eaters had spiny backs or armoured sides, and some meat-eaters had bulldog-like faces and arms even shorter than *T. rex*'s.

**Patagonia – Today** Here, in two sites about 160 kilometres apart, the world's biggest meat-eating and plant-eating dinosaurs were recently discovered. Above, scientists excavate an *Argentinosaurus* vertebra.

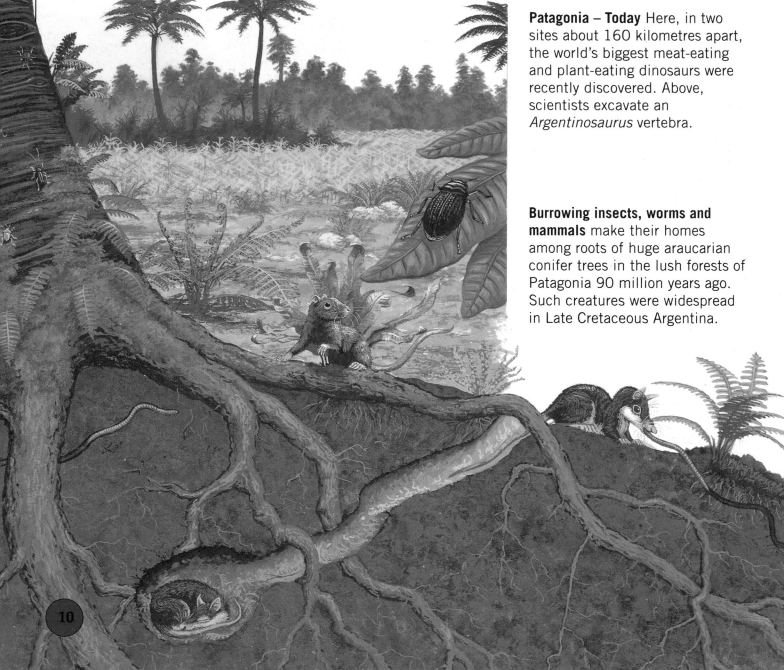

**Burrowing insects, worms and mammals** make their homes among roots of huge araucarian conifer trees in the lush forests of Patagonia 90 million years ago. Such creatures were widespread in Late Cretaceous Argentina.

South America was an island continent for much of the Cretaceous Period. As a result, the dinosaurs of that continent went their own peculiar direction in evolution. In the Northern Hemisphere, by the Late Cretaceous, horned and duck-billed dinosaurs had replaced the giant plant-eating sauropods of the Jurassic Period. But in South America the giant sauropods were still thriving. They were members of a large and stocky group known as the titanosaurs.

Predators were also huge in South America about 90 million years ago. In the Northern Hemisphere, small raptor dinosaurs were widespread (see pages 23 and 26–27), and bigger hunters, the tyrannosaurs, were soon to appear. However, in South America, the killer giants that have just been discovered were even larger and bulkier than *Tyrannosaurus* (see page 42), but they had less powerful jaws.

(see pages 23 and 26–27)

(see page 42)

## FACT FILE

**Patagonia, Then and Now**
Patagonia, in present-day southern South America, was not as far south 90 million years ago as it is today. The climate was warmer and moister than today's windy deserts. In the Early Cretaceous, South America was still part of Gondwana. By the Late Cretaceous, it had become a separate continent.

**ANIMALS**
1. *Argentinosaurus* (ARE-jen-TEEN-o-SAW-rus)
2. Descendant of *Giganotosaurus* (JY-ga-NO-toe-SAW-rus)
3. Pterosaur (TAIR-o-SAW)

**PLANTS**
4. Araucarian conifer (AR-aw-CARE-ee-un)
5. Ferns
6. *Gunnera* (GUN-er-a)

ALSO AT THIS SITE:
Small mammals
Cycadeoids (sy-KAD-ee-oyds)
Cycads (SY-kads)

### Patagonia – Then
Several *Argentinosaurus* – the largest known dinosaur – nibble at the branches of the towering araucarian trees, deep in the well-watered evergreen forests of central Argentina. Huge, but more lightly built, sauropods, possibly relatives of *Diplodocus*, feed here, too. The plant-eaters' diet includes ferns and the leaves of flowering plants like *Gunnera*.

Suddenly, a meat-eater – perhaps a descendant of the huge killer *Giganotosaurus* – darts out from the thick vegetation. With large blade-like teeth suitable for slicing flesh (not crushing bone), it homes in on one of the herbivores as a target. Small mammals lurk in the distance among ferns, out of harm's way. A pterosaur glides overhead, on its way to the coast in search of fish.

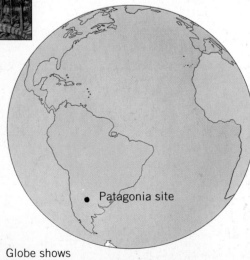

Globe shows
the position of the continents now.

Patagonia site

# THE BIGGEST EVER

These record-setting dinosaurs are truly awe-inspiring. Imagine a plant-eater as long as three school buses and taller than a house. And picture a meat-eater as long as a removal van, with a head bigger than a whole human!

The giant dinosaurs of Patagonia showed several features that were unknown on other dinosaurs. The enormous plant-eaters had an extra set of supports on each of their vertebrae, which were as tall as a grown human and as wide as a refrigerator. These bony braces would have helped contain their huge guts.

Twenty million years after the giant plant- and meat-eaters ruled South America, the continent was home to dinosaurs half as large but still strange. The spiny manes on some of these huge plant-eaters and the large horns over the eyes of the meat-eaters may have been developed for display. These prominent bones could have been used to attract the attention of possible mates or to inspire fear in rivals (see page 32).

## GIGANOTOSAURUS
**Meaning of name:** 'Giant southern reptile'
**Order:** Saurischia
**Size, Weight:** 13.5 metres long, 8 tonnes or more
**Location:** Argentina
**Diet:** Meat

*Giganotosaurus* was named in 1995. It is known from a single specimen, more than three-quarters complete. This dinosaur, with its large teeth, was a terrifying hunter. It was probably faster and more alert than the plant-eaters in its world. It was narrower in the shoulders than *Tyrannosaurus*, but longer and more heavily built.

*Giganotosaurus* was succeeded by smaller but still impressive meat-eating dinosaurs that ruled Late Cretaceous South America.

GIGANOTOSAURUS

*Giganotosaurus* (shown in light blue in this comparison) was bigger than *Tyrannosaurus rex* (shown in dark blue) but it was not so powerful. It had a smaller brain, less powerful jaws and narrower teeth than *T. rex* had.

*T. rex* was long considered by palaeontologists as the all-time king of predators. For killing power, it still is unrivaled. But *Giganotosaurus* is now the largest carnivorous dinosaur known. It was a long as four cars.

# PLANTS

*Gunnera* today has leaves 2 metres long. The leaves are fan-shaped like those of a rhubarb plant. But in Late Cretaceous Argentina, these flowering plants grew far smaller, with leaves just 10 centimetres across. Prominent among the flowering plants of the time were shrubs with magnolia-like flowers like those shown below (and on page 31).

MAGNOLIA-LIKE FLOWERS

*ARGENTINOSAURUS*

## ARGENTINOSAURUS

**Meaning of name:** 'Argentina lizard'
**Order:** Saurischia
**Size, Weight:** 33.5 metres long, 100 tonnes or more
**Location:** Argentina
**Diet:** Plants

*Argentinosaurus* may be the heaviest animal ever to walk the Earth, three times heavier than *Seismosaurus* (although not as long). Scientists discovered only a few fossils of *Argentinosaurus*, including one shin and bits of the hips, backbone and ribs (see page 10). This dinosaur was very solidly built and designed to support great weight. Its vertebrae, each 1.5 metres long and 1.5 metres wide, had extra bony struts linking them. Most dinosaur ribs are flattened, but *Argentinosaurus*'s were stout and rounded.

# BULLDOZING THE HABITAT

Soft mudstone around the fossilized *Giganotosaurus* suggests that its habitat was a lush river delta. The nearby *Argentinosaurus* site is harder sandstone, with pebbles surrounding the bones. These fossils indicate that by *Argentinosaurus*'s time, just a few million years later, this nearby area was one of faster-flowing rivers.

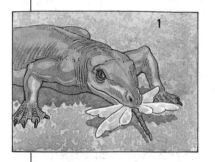

**FOOD CHAIN**
Plants are consumed by plant-eating insects, reptiles and mammals. Here a lizard **(1)** feeds on an insect.

A small mammal kills and eats the lizard **(2)**. The mammal, in turn, is preyed on by a bird **(3)** while it rests after its meal.

In all environments, life-forms survive by eating other organisms. The link among living things that eat one another is known as a food chain. In Patagonia, as in other Late Cretaceous lands, carnivorous dinosaurs were at the top of each food chain. But the length of the food chains varied greatly. The giant plant-eating dinosaurs like *Argentinosaurus* were probably in a very short chain: they ate plants and usually died of disease, injury or old age.

Of course, the plant-eating dinosaurs were part of a web of interlinked food chains. Some of the carnivores shown in the food chain above preyed on many kinds of plant-eaters.

In the savannas of modern Africa, elephants are part of a food chain that can be as short as that involving *Argentinosaurus*. Elephants eat leaves and branches of trees. Eventually they die, or occasionally the old, infirm or young are the victims of large predators such as lions.

Surprised, the small bird is no match for the agile meat-eating dinosaur **(4)** that overpowers it.

*Giganotosaurus* **(5)** snaps up the smaller meat-eater. It would also have fed on the flesh of plant-eaters.

Although they return many nutrients to the soil through their waste and their decaying corpses, big plant-eaters can also cause great damage to plant life as they feed. Unless elephants roam widely, they can quickly destroy all the trees in an area. The same was probably true of giant plant-eating dinosaurs.

**Seen from above,** *Argentinosaurus* crushes smaller trees as it feeds on an araucarian tree (left). Pterosaurs glide overhead. Small meat-eating dinosaurs hunt in the shadow of the giant.

**Elephants are the largest plant-eaters** in modern Africa. To satisfy their huge appetites, they uproot trees or strip them bare. Confined to a limited area, they may destroy all vegetation.

**Ninety million years ago, browsing** *Argentinosaurus* left a path of destruction. But these dinosaurs might have moved on to new feeding areas without destroying all the trees in any region.

# DIFFICULT DIGGING

The discoveries of the largest meat-eating and plant-eating dinosaurs ever known were made by amateur fossil-hunters in northern Patagonia. Much remains to be learned about these creatures and their habitats. Excavation of the largest of them all, *Argentinosaurus*, has been going on during several recent summers.

## DEATH OF AN *ARGENTINOSAURUS*

*Argentinosaurus* dies (1) and falls into a fast-flowing river. Sand from the bottom of the river, along with many pebbles, builds up quickly around the body.

**Left:** Professor Rodolfo Coria (on the right) and an assistant clean the fossil skull of a big meat-eater.
**Below:** Working at one site, Coria's team has excavated huge bones of *Argentinosaurus* including the pelvis, backbones and leg bone shown in the illustration. They recently discovered more of this dinosaur's fossils nearby.

A rancher found the 1.5-metre-long shinbone of *Argentinosaurus* in 1987. It was beside a road near his home in Plaza Huincul. At first he guessed it was a petrified tree log and showed it to local scientists. They reasoned from its shape and porous internal structure that it was a dinosaur bone. They called in fossil experts from Buenos Aires, Argentina's capital. José Bonaparte, a palaeontologist from the national science museum, led a full-scale excavation.

The dig at the site uncovered 1.5-metre-long vertebrae and parts of *Argentinosaurus*'s hip. Professor Bonaparte's assistant, Rodolfo Coria, stayed on in Plaza Huincul to continue the work. He has found more bones of *Argentinosaurus*, including a small portion of its skull. Professor Coria has also excavated many other dinosaur fossils in the region, including *Giganotosaurus* (see page 12).

**The bones of the *Argentinosaurus*** are picked clean of muscle and blood vessels by small scavenging dinosaurs (2). The bone heap causes a sandbank to form in the riverbed. The swift-flowing water carries down more rocks, which wedge in the sandbank. The current washes away many of the smaller bones or scatters them along the riverbed.

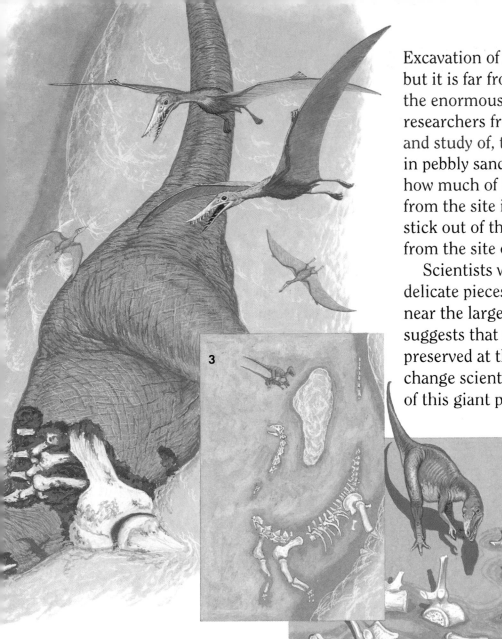

Excavation of *Argentinosaurus* began in 1988, but it is far from finished. Lack of funds and the enormous labour involved have slowed researchers from completing their search for, and study of, the bones. Each vertebra, covered in pebbly sandstone, weighs nearly a tonne. Just how much of the dinosaur will be recovered from the site is not yet known. Pieces of bone stick out of the ground as much as 200 metres from the site of the first discoveries.

Scientists were surprised to discover small, delicate pieces of jawbone of *Argentinosaurus* near the larger bones in 1995. This discovery suggests that much of the dinosaur is still preserved at the site. New finds may well change scientists' image and understanding of this giant prehistoric animal.

**In 1988, Argentinian scientists** excavate the *Argentinosaurus* site **(5)**. Air-powered drills are used to expose the bones. Other fossils can be seen in the ground, but the work is so difficult and slow that many bones have yet to be excavated.

**At the original spot** where the dinosaur died, only the heaviest bones **(3)** remain after just a few years of battering from the river current. The largest vertebrae and the sacrum (hipbone) are so heavy that even the fast waters do not tumble them downstream.

A small theropod dinosaur looks in the shallow river for the last bits of decaying flesh on the bones of *Argentinosaurus* before sand and pebbles cover them **(4)**. The bones become fossils as minerals enter into them and they harden.

Over millions of years, the fossilized bones of the *Argentinosaurus* become buried deeper in the rocks.

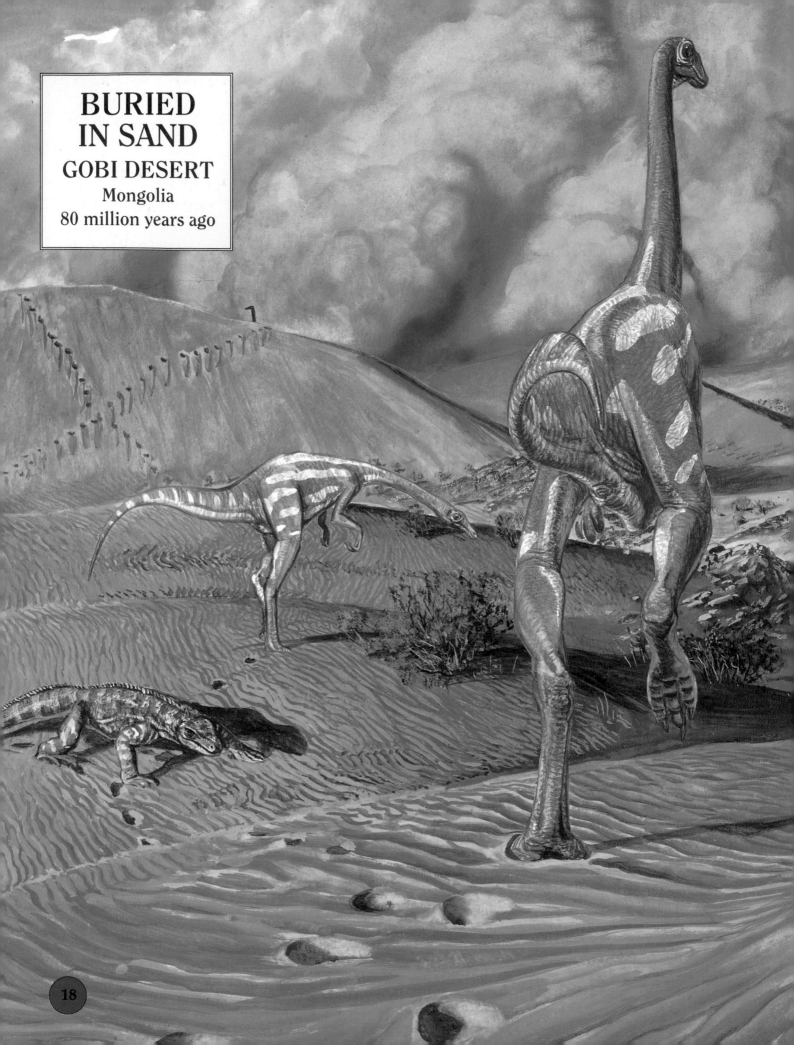

A nesting beaked dinosaur feeds a lizard to its newly hatched youngsters, unaware of the fast-approaching sandstorm. Ostrich-like ornithomimid dinosaurs and other desert-dwellers journey in search of scattered sources of food and water.

# SHIFTING SANDS

Spectacular dinosaurs lived in Central Asia 80 million years ago. Their habitat was a dry, sometimes desert-like, environment. The soft sands of the Gobi Desert preserved fossils so well that we know a great deal about Central Asian dinosaurs at that time. The first nests of dinosaurs were found here, with tiny babies and embryos inside.

North America and Asia were connected during much of the Cretaceous Period. Not surprisingly, the many fossil finds in the Gobi Desert include dinosaurs like those found in North America. But there are also many unusual creatures known from this region: big lizards, dome-headed herbivores and giant sauropod dinosaurs. Missing from this area are the large horned dinosaurs like *Triceratops*, so common in Late Cretaceous North America. The sands of the Gobi preserved outstanding fossils of other creatures, too, from burrowing insects to mammals.

Plants that adapted to dry conditions are also found as fossils here. The Gobi is even drier now than when dinosaurs lived there.

**Gobi Desert – Today** The Gobi is a crescent-shaped stretch of land nearly 1,600 kilometres wide in central Asia. Its climate varies from freezing to extremely hot. Divided between China and Mongolia, the desert is mostly barren and dunes are rare.

**A large theropod** runs across the desert. The dung it leaves behind attracts dung beetles that bury the waste as food for their young. Other insects crawl on the desert surface. A hidden world of animals lives underground, such as beetles, worms and centipedes. Here they are protected from the harsh environment.

But these insects are not completely safe underground. Spiders prey upon them. Their homes can be destroyed by a falling sand dune or the step of a dinosaur.

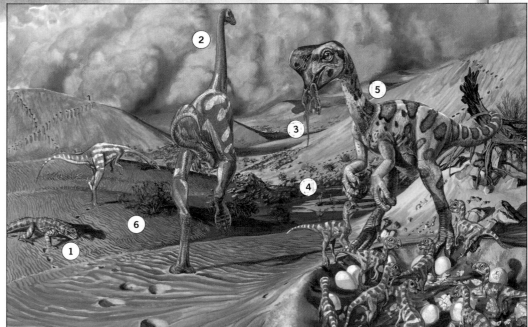

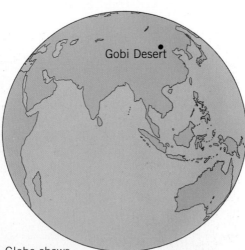

Mongolia was home to nearly one in five of all the meat-eating dinosaurs known.

**ANIMALS**
1. *Estesia* (ess-TEE-zee-ah)
2. *Gallimimus* (GAL-ih-MY-mus)
3. Lizard
4. *Mononykus* (MAW-no-NY-kus)
5. *Oviraptor* (O-vih-RAP-tur)

**PLANTS**
6. *Ephedra* (eh-FED-rah)

ALSO AT THIS SITE:
*Protoceratops* (PRO-toe-SAIR-uh-tops)
*Saurornithoides* (SAWR-or-nith-OY-deez)
*Tylocephale* (TIE-luh-SEF-uh-lee)
Velociraptor (veh-LAW-sih-RAP-tur)
*Dalembya* (DAH-lem-BEE-yuh)
*Kirengeshoma* (ky-REN-guh-SHOW-mah)

**Mongolia, Then and Now**
Asia today looks much as it did 80 million years ago. But in the Late Cretaceous, sea levels were higher than they are now, and the Gobi was more humid, with shallow ponds and lakes during the wet season.

Globe shows the position of the continents now.

## Gobi Desert – Then

An *Oviraptor* feeds its nestlings with a small lizard it has caught. An ostrich-like *Gallimimus*, one of the fastest of all dinosaurs, runs off towards a stream while another *Gallimimus* looks on. A group of small birds, *Mononykus*, drink from the stream. A large lizard, *Estesia*, slithers along the ground.

The sparse vegetation of Late Cretaceous Mongolia included the shrub-like *Dalembya*; the bare-looking, weedy *Ephedra*; and the *Kirengeshoma* plant, with its shield-shaped leaves. These were food for dome-headed pachycephalosaurs, *Tylocephale*, and small-horned dinosaurs such as *Protoceratops*.

# LONG LEGS, DOME HEADS

The dinosaurs that lived in Mongolia 80 million years ago included some of the most intelligent and fastest-moving dinosaurs of all time. The resemblance to birds of some of these dinosaurs, particularly the lightly built meat-eaters, is striking. The bird-like Mongolian dinosaurs were not ancestors of birds. Birds had evolved from dinosaurs in the Late Jurassic Period or even earlier.

*GALLIMIMUS*
**Meaning of name:** 'Chicken mimic'
**Order:** Saurischia
**Size, Weight:** 5 metres long, about 225 kilos
**Location:** Mongolia
**Diet:** Small animals and insects

*Gallimimus* had a long tail and a snout shaped like a goose's bill.

**The skeletons of *Gallimimus*** and ostriches have much in common. Both are long-legged, with hollow-boned and lightly built bodies. Some wrist and skull bones are also similar.

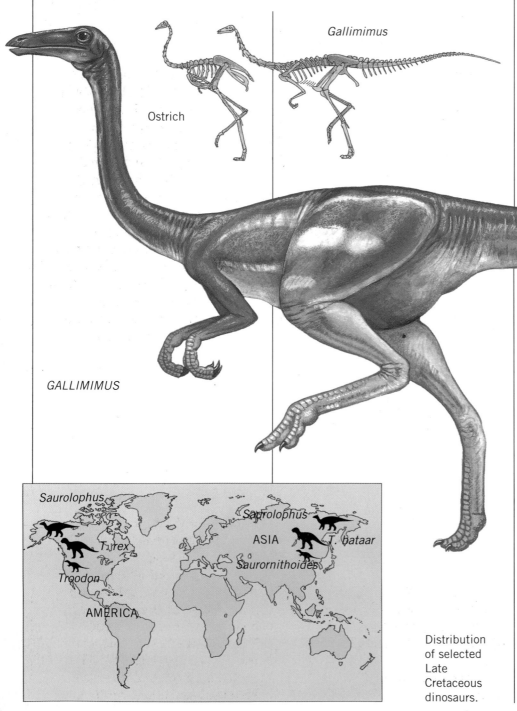

Ostrich

Gallimimus

GALLIMIMUS

**Many closely related animals** lived in Asia and North America when these two landmasses were linked in the Late Cretaceous. Despite very different climates, the two continents shared nearly identical dinosaur meat-eaters, from tyrannosaurs to raptors and ostrich-like speedsters. Duck-billed, domed, and small horned dinosaurs are also known from both continents. Large horned dinosaurs appear to have been absent from Asia. They may have needed a climate or type of food not available there.

**The map shows** *Tyrannosaurus rex* had a cousin in Asia called *Tyrannosaurus bataar*. The meat-eater *Troodon* of North America had an Asian 'twin' called *Saurornithoides*. *Saurolophus*, a duckbill, lived on both continents.

Saurolophus
Saurolophus
T. rex
ASIA
T. bataar
Saurornithoides
Troodon
AMERICA

Distribution of selected Late Cretaceous dinosaurs.

# PLANTS

Flowering plants became the dominant form of vegetation by the Late Cretaceous Period, at least in the Northern Hemisphere. In the Gobi, plant life was sparse in most places because there was little water.

But several kinds of flowering plants and trees are known from this region 80 million years ago. They include a climbing plant called *Kirengeshoma*, which had little oak-leaf-shaped leaves hanging down from the top of it. *Ephedra*, known as Mormon tea, was a shrub with climbing stick-like branches. *Ephedra* grows in dry climates today, such as those in Utah and in the Middle East.

**Ephedra growing in scrubland in Israel.** It also grows beside the Wailing Wall in Jerusalem.

**SKULL**

*Oviraptor*'s skull was deep, with a high crest, but very light in weight. It had two teeth in its upper jaw, and it had a large beak.

*OVIRAPTOR*

*TYLOCEPHALE*

**TYLOCEPHALE**
**Meaning of name:** 'Swollen head'
**Order:** Ornithischia
**Size, Weight:** 2 metres long, 55 kilos
**Location:** Mongolia
**Diet:** Plants

*OVIRAPTOR*
**Meaning of name:** 'Egg thief'
**Order:** Saurischia·
**Size, Weight:** 1.8 metres long or longer, 22.5 to 40 kilos
**Location:** Mongolia
**Diet:** Meat

*Oviraptor* was lightly built and had a wishbone. This bone is common in birds but not in dinosaurs. *Oviraptor* had large three-fingered hands with strong claws and three toes on each foot. It had just two teeth, but it may have been a good hunter. Remains of lizards near the stomach area of *Oviraptor* suggest it ate these reptiles. It may also have crushed eggs with its beak.

Dome-headed dinosaurs are known from both Mongolia and North America in the Late Cretaceous. *Tylocephale* is one of several smaller dome-headed dinosaurs from Mongolia. Only a part of a broken skull has been found. The skull was 10 centimetres thick and 12.5 centimetres high. The domed head is thought to have been used for butting rivals.

23

# HEAT AND DROUGHT

Near the end of the Mesozoic Era, as today, Mongolia was a place of great extremes. Nights were cool, but the midday heat was blazing. Water and plants were scarce. Wind-driven sandstorms could rage for weeks at a time. Sand dunes might suddenly collapse, suffocating unsuspecting animals.

Today in the Gobi Desert, animals travel far to find water and are adapted to going great distances without drinking. Some are nocturnal, avoiding the hot, dry days by becoming active only at night. Others, such as foxes, have large ears that act like radiators to help cool them in the heat.

How did dinosaurs cope with hot desert life? Perhaps many travelled and fed by night. Many, though not all, of the Gobi dinosaurs were small. Perhaps they could not find enough food to support a large body size. The stress of desert life favoured small animals. Certainly, the quick, smart and lightly built predators like *Velociraptor* and *Saurornithoides* (see page 27) were well equipped to kill small animals. They may have been pack hunters and taken on larger prey. Whatever the cause of their comparatively small size, the horned dinosaurs of the Gobi Desert grew no bigger than dogs, whereas in North America some were as much as 5 metres long.

**Two-humped Bactrian camels rest in the Gobi Desert today.** Camels are the most famous of desert-living creatures. These animals, renowned for their ability to travel many days without water, draw nutrients from the fatty humps on their backs. Camels are also unusually adapted to reduce the amount of water lost from their bodies through breathing, sweating and urination. And their thick, woolly fur blocks the entry of daytime heat.

Other animals today use a variety of strategies to cope with desert life. Many desert animals, such as the coyote, come out to hunt only at dawn, dusk and night. Birds make their homes inside water-holding cactus.

**In the moonlight of the Gobi** small mammals scurry around a hollow tree. A pack of *Saurornithoides* scans a nesting site in the distance. Perhaps the meat-eaters are gathering for an attack, using their superior eyesight, speed and intelligence to hunt plant-eaters in the dim light.

*Velociraptor* and *Oviraptor* were small but had especially large eyes (see pages 26–27). They may have hunted in twilight and moonlight to make the most of their superior vision. Lightly built, they were faster and more agile than the surrounding plant-eaters. They were also large-brained, which suggests they may have hunted in packs. *Saurornithoides* had a plum-sized brain and a slender, 2-metre-long body. Comparing body weight to brain size, scientists estimate this dinosaur was one of the most intelligent, perhaps as smart as some birds today.

**Dinosaurs and other animals** in the Gobi Desert 80 million years ago coped with hot, dry weather. Small mammals may have burrowed under rocks or in the ground until the cool night. But large dinosaurs could not hide from the heat. Perhaps they slept at midday in the shade of the gnarled trees that were around, as kangaroos do today.

Desert-dwelling reptiles today conserve water. Their scaly skins keep water in and they lose little water in their thick, pasty urine. Gobi dinosaurs may have functioned in the same way.

**To avoid the midday heat,** a *Gallimimus* **(1)** hides in the shade of a tree, while two *Velociraptor* **(2)** lie curled up in shadow behind a dune.

Mammals rest in dens underground **(3)**, and small reptiles and many insects burrow under rocks until the cool night arrives.

# WHOSE NEST?

In 1923, American Museum of Natural History scientists found the first known dinosaur nests in the Gobi (see page 5). The eggs were thought to belong to the plant-eater *Protoceratops*. The skeleton of a toothless meat-eater was found on top of one of the nests. It was named *Oviraptor,* 'the egg thief'.

In 1993, scientists from the same museum uncovered a nest in the Gobi with similar shaped eggs. Some of these eggs contained embryos. The embryos proved to be bones of unhatched *Oviraptor*. *Oviraptor* was not an egg thief. It was an egg-laying parent, killed on top of its nest.

**Chinese scientists dig for dinosaur bones in the Gobi Desert,** near the site where American scientists first found the fossils of *Protoceratops*, *Oviraptor* and dinosaur eggs in the early 1920s. The Chinese scientists uncovered many more dinosaur eggs as well as some materials left behind by the previous expedition.

## *OVIRAPTOR* AS PARENT

*Oviraptor* may have sat directly on its eggs **(1)** to incubate them, as most birds do. Or it might have made a mound of plants over the eggs to keep them warm, as some reptiles and a few birds do today.
A dozen or more eggs, shaped like small loaves of French bread, were arranged in a spiral within the nest. As some of the chicks hatched, or even before, the *Oviraptor* may have had to leave the nest to feed. Perhaps it brought back food for its helpless young.

Here, the *Oviraptor* leaves the nest to try to frighten off a pack of very young *Velociraptor* **(2)**. As youngsters, these swift and smart hunters may have been real egg thieves. As adults, *Velociraptor* were capable of hunting big lizards and other prey.

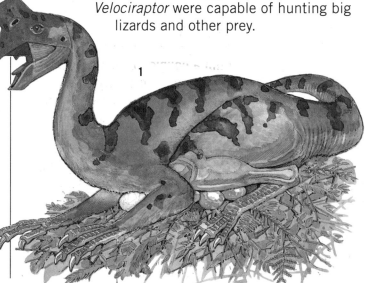

**Few fossil finds** reveal the actual moment of death of prehistoric creatures. But the find known as 'The Fighting Dinosaurs' (above) shows the horned dinosaur *Protoceratops* and *Velociraptor* grappling as a sand dune collapsed upon them. The fossils were found by Polish scientists who explored the Gobi Desert from 1963 to 1971.

One dramatic find by the Andrews team was a meat-eating dinosaur the size of a large dog, with huge toe and hand claws. They called this lightly built long-legged hunter *Velociraptor*, 'swift robber'. It was one of the smallest raptor dinosaurs. The first raptors were as large as lorries. But Late Cretaceous raptors like *Velociraptor* and *Dromaeosaurus* (in North America) were small. *Velociraptor* was fast. It leaped into the air to slash its prey with its 10-centimetre-long second-finger and toe claws.

In the movie *Jurassic Park*, *Velociraptor* was portrayed as a pack hunter, with the speed of a cheetah and the intelligence of a chimpanzee. In reality, it was more likely as fast as a poodle. Although it was smarter than any mammal or dinosaur of its time, it fell far short of the brain power of a chimpanzee. There is no fossil evidence yet to show conclusively that *Velociraptor* travelled in packs.

3

The *Oviraptor* is set upon by a pack of young and tiny *Velociraptor* **(3)**. They leap at the *Oviraptor*, slashing it with their hand and toe claws, and biting it with their sharp teeth.

But the young predators are too small to be a serious threat to the full-grown *Oviraptor*. It brushes some away with its tail and arms, and kills two of them by biting off their heads.

4

After chewing the baby *Velociraptor* to make it easier to digest, the *Oviraptor* will feed the meat to its young in the nest **(4)**. The youngsters eagerly await their meal of raptor meat.

**Within a couple of metres of the *Oviraptor* nest** of embryos and eggs, scientists discovered two crushed *Velociraptor* skulls. These skulls were scarcely 2.5 centimetres long and must have come from youngsters. The scenes shown on these pages offer one explanation of how the isolated and broken skulls of these *Velociraptor* babies might have come to be found so near the *Oviraptor* nest.

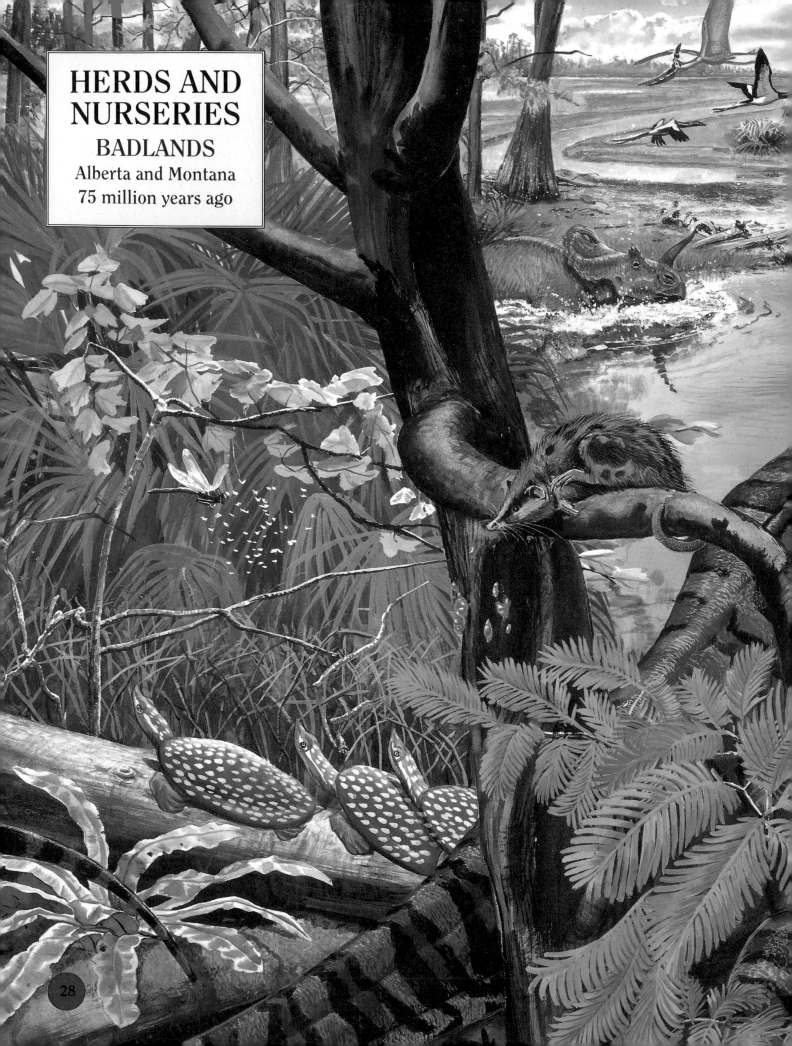

Along the lush banks of a river, a duck-billed dinosaur is startled by the approach of a big meat-eater. Insects, turtles and mammals move among the tree branches and leaves. Birds and pterosaurs share the sky, while flowering plants compete with ferns to fill the damp ground round the trees.

# DINOSAUR NURSERY

The rocks from the badlands of North America show us a time, 75 million years ago, when this was a lush, sub-tropical land. Small plant-eating dinosaurs nested beside the great colonies of duck-billed dinosaurs. Herds of horned dinosaurs roamed the countryside. Predatory dinosaurs, crocodilians, pterosaurs, birds and little mammals lived amid many flowering and evergreen plants.

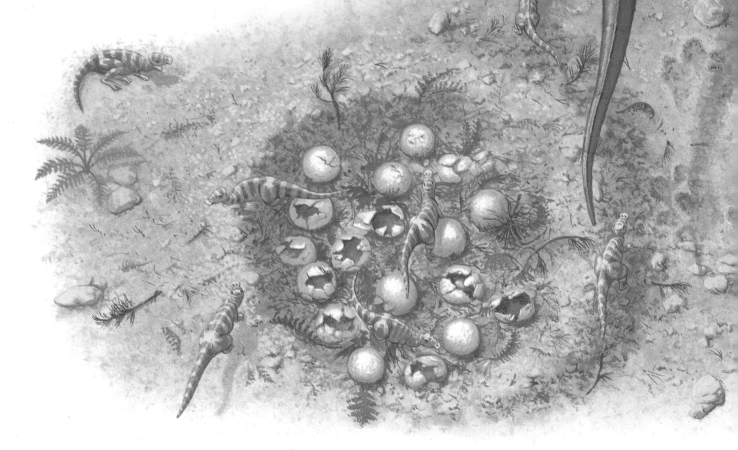

**Badlands – Today**
Devil's Coulee in Alberta, Canada, lies in the heart of badlands. These cliffs were created by rivers that vanished a few thousand years ago. Seventy-five million years ago this land was a lush river delta, full of nesting dinosaurs. Nests of duck-billed dinosaurs are found in nearby Montana, too.

**Newly hatched duck-billed dinosaurs** explore the area around their nest. The tiny dinosaurs still inside the eggs peck away with their egg teeth (see page 35) at the hard shell. Some eggs are cracking. A duckbill parent leaves the nest to find food. Parents may have regurgitated partially digested plants as food for their hungry young.

Like many birds, some dinosaurs might have been devoted parents that watched over their helpless young and brought them food in the nest. One scientist, Dr John Horner, sparked excitement over this idea in the late 1970s. In Montana, he discovered the fossils of a new type of dinosaur, which he named *Maiasaura* ('good mother lizard'). Among other clues, he found the bones of hatchlings and juveniles lying together in and around their nests. He thinks the hatchlings stayed in the nest for weeks while their parents fed and protected them.

Other newly hatched dinosaurs were up and running immediately and needed little parental attention. Evidence for both of these styles of bringing up baby dinosaurs has been claimed from fossils found in the North American West.

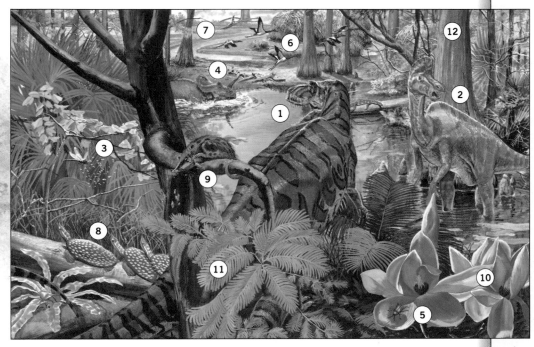

## FACT FILE

**Badlands, Then and Now** The badlands now have cold winters and hot, dry summers. In the Late Cretaceous, the Alberta badlands were wet lowlands. They are now prairie. The Montana badlands are in the foothills of the Rocky Mountains. In the Late Cretaceous, this area was a dry but fertile upland.

### ANIMALS

1. *Albertosaurus* (al-BERT-o-SAW-rus)
2. *Corythosaurus* (kor-ITH-o-SAW-rus)
3. Dragonflies and midges
4. *Centrosaurus* (SEN-tro-SAW-rus)
5. Leaf beetles
6. *Presbyornis* bird (PRESS-bee-OR-nis)
7. *Pteranodon* (tair-AN-o-don)
8. *Trionyx* (try-ON-icks)
9. Unnamed mammal

### PLANTS

10. Magnolia-like shrub
11. *Metasequoia* (MET-a-si-KOY-a) conifer
12. *Taxodium* (tax-OH-dee-um) conifer

ALSO AT THIS SITE:
*Hypacrosaurus* (hy-PACK-ro-SAW-rus)
*Maiasaura* (MY-a-SAW-ra)
*Orodromeus* (OR-o-DRO-mee-us)

Globe shows
the position of the continents now.

## Badlands – Then

An *Albertosaurus*, a large predator of Late Cretaceous Alberta and Montana, roams in search of prey, alive and dead. Among its victims may be duck-billed dinosaurs such as *Corythosaurus* or a horned dinosaur like *Centrosaurus*. These herbivores feast on the twigs of trees much like modern redwood and cypress conifers.

Little mammals scurry along the branches looking for midges, dragonflies and beetles to eat.

*Trionyx* turtles that basked in the sun earlier in the day now cool off in the shade of the forest. Birds and enormous pterosaurs fly overhead.

In drier areas a few hundred miles away, duckbills called *Maiasaura* and *Hypacrosaurus* build nests and lay eggs. Other dinosaurs living in these areas include various kinds with horns, some with dome-shaped heads, others with thick, protective armoured skin, and many kinds of small meat-eaters.

# CAN·D·'S FOSSIL T·E·SURES

More kinds of dinosaurs are known from Alberta 75 million years ago than from any other time and place. Huge numbers of duck-billed and horned dinosaurs have been found there. These types dominated western North America from 75 million to 65 million years ago. While duckbills were successful around the world at this time, large horned dinosaurs, such as *Triceratops* and *Centrosaurus,* are known only from North America.

The horned giants of North America sported a variety of frill and horn designs. It is uncertain whether these horns were ever used as defence against predators. But holes found in the heavy skulls indicate that the horns were used in battles among rival horned dinosaurs.

## INSECTS

*Cretonomyia* is a fly that lives today and also existed 75 million years ago. A specimen was preserved when the living fly was trapped inside a glob of sticky pine sap in Alberta, Canada, between 83 million and 75 million years ago. The sap hardened into a piece of amber, with the dead insect preserved inside.

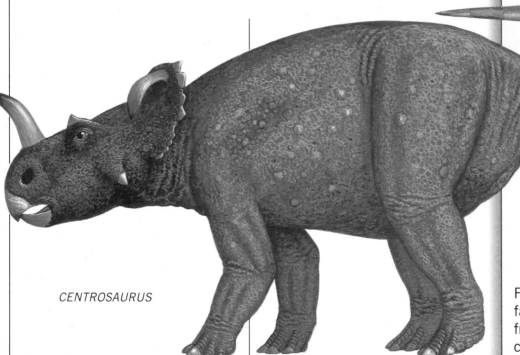

*CENTROSAURUS*

*CENTROSAURUS*
**Meaning of name:** 'Sharp-pointed lizard'
**Order:** Ornithischia
**Size, Weight:** 5 metres long, 1 to 2 tonnes
**Location:** Alberta
**Diet:** Plants

*Centrosaurus* is one of the most decorated of all horned dinosaurs.

Its head frill had a thick edge, two hooks that pointed backwards and two horns that curved forwards. *Centrosaurus*'s crest was notched with sharp edges. On some individuals the nose horn curved forwards, while on others it stood straight up or curved backwards. The differences in nose horn sizes and shapes may relate both to the age and the sex of the individual.

Flies of the *Cretonomyia* family are known today only from Australia. They cannot cross oceans and could not have crossed the Pacific from Canada 75 million years ago. Since ancient preserved *Cretonomyia* specimens have been found in both Australia and Canada, the flies must have evolved more than 130 million years ago when the world's continents were still closely linked.

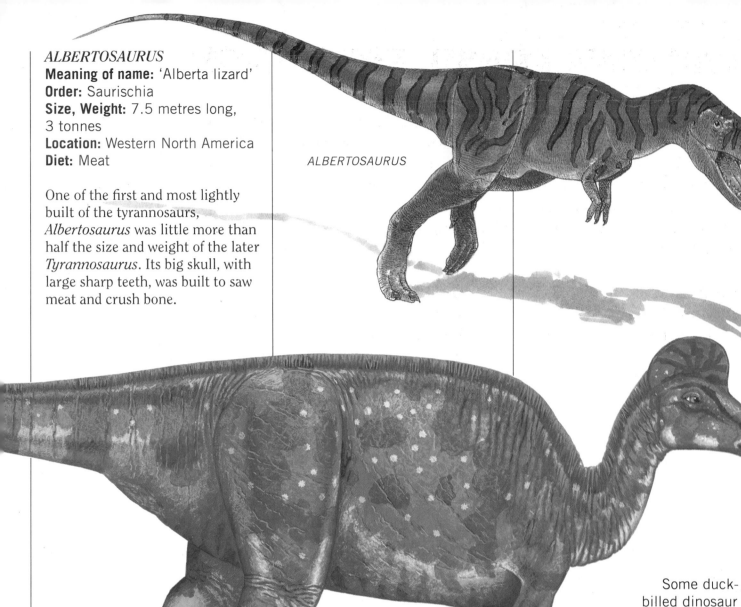

## ALBERTOSAURUS

**Meaning of name:** 'Alberta lizard'
**Order:** Saurischia
**Size, Weight:** 7.5 metres long, 3 tonnes
**Location:** Western North America
**Diet:** Meat

One of the first and most lightly built of the tyrannosaurs, *Albertosaurus* was little more than half the size and weight of the later *Tyrannosaurus*. Its big skull, with large sharp teeth, was built to saw meat and crush bone.

*ALBERTOSAURUS*

*HYPACROSAURUS*

It was distinguishable from *Corythosaurus* by its ridged back and shorter head.

## HYPACROSAURUS

**Meaning of name:** 'Almost the highest lizard'
**Order:** Ornithischia
**Size, Weight:** 9 metres long, 2 to 3 tonnes
**Locations:** Alberta and Montana
**Diet:** Plants

*Hypacrosaurus* was a duck-billed dinosaur of the dry uplands. Its relative, *Corythosaurus*, lived in wetter lowlands. *Hypacrosaurus* is one of the small number of dinosaurs for which scientists have fossil eggs.

Duckbills had short toothless beaks, used for snipping off plants. They also had many rows of small flat teeth for grinding. There were nearly forty rows of these teeth in each of *Hypacrosaurus*'s large jaws.

Some duck-billed dinosaur fossil skulls have no head crests, while others have elaborate tubes or helmet-shaped domes. The long nasal tubes may have been used to send low-frequency sounds. Elephants and whales make such sounds to send messages over long distances.

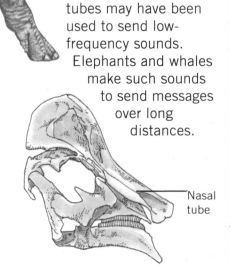

Nasal tube

# THE NESTING SCENE

The nesting colonies of duck-billed dinosaurs found in Alberta and Montana have much in common with colonies of seabirds today. Huge numbers of animals build their nests in a crowded community. The large tightly packed group offers defence against predators that might eat the eggs or young chicks.

*Maiasaura* duckbills might have cared for their young as birds do. Their nests contained crushed eggshells and a lump of half-digested plants was nearby. Some scientists think that *Maiasaura* hatchlings stayed in the nest, crushing their eggshells as they moved around, and that adults made baby food by spitting up chewed plants. Other scientists think the settling earth crushed the eggshells and preserved a lump of chewed nest-building material. The search is on for more clues.

*Maiasaura* nests contained a dozen or more eggs. The size of the embryos at hatching is not known, though *Maiasaura* bones of individuals thought to be less than 30 centimetres long have been found.

**Birds circle over the nest site,** looking for stray hatchling *Orodromeus* to catch and eat.

**This nesting colony,** like that found at Egg Mountain in Choteau, Montana, belongs to long-legged little dinosaurs known as *Orodromeus* ('mountain runner'). Eggs were laid in a spiral in the nest, which was a mound of mud packed by an adult. The eggs might have been covered with vegetation and adults might have attended the nests. Each nest was separated from the next by the body length of an adult – about 2 metres. These baby plant-eaters could run immediately after hatching.

**Two *Orodromeus* parents watch over their nests,** which they have covered with plant material probably to incubate the eggs and perhaps to hide them from predators. Others busily gather materials to complete their own nests.

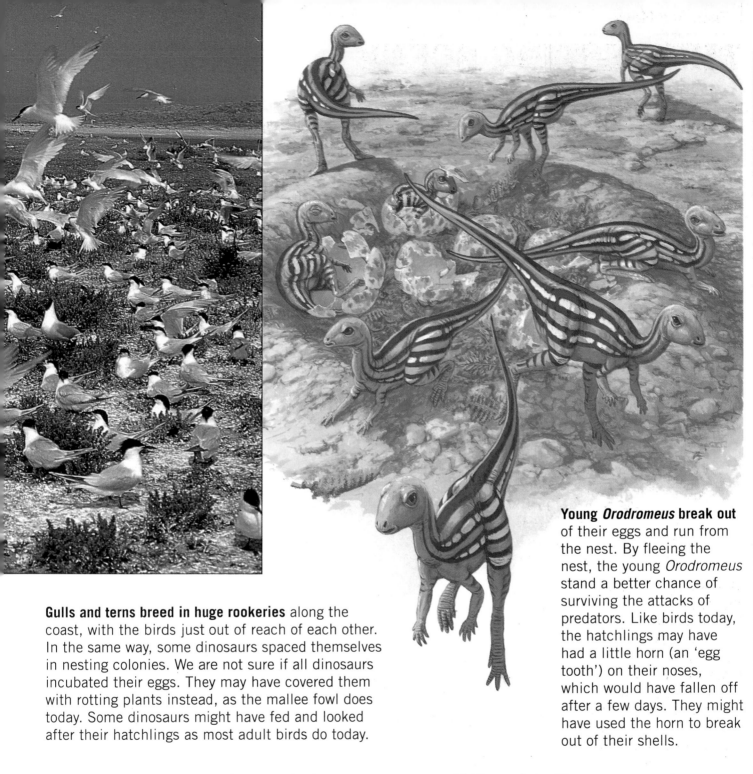

**Young *Orodromeus* break out** of their eggs and run from the nest. By fleeing the nest, the young *Orodromeus* stand a better chance of surviving the attacks of predators. Like birds today, the hatchlings may have had a little horn (an 'egg tooth') on their noses, which would have fallen off after a few days. They might have used the horn to break out of their shells.

**Gulls and terns breed in huge rookeries** along the coast, with the birds just out of reach of each other. In the same way, some dinosaurs spaced themselves in nesting colonies. We are not sure if all dinosaurs incubated their eggs. They may have covered them with rotting plants instead, as the mallee fowl does today. Some dinosaurs might have fed and looked after their hatchlings as most adult birds do today.

Small dinosaurs like *Orodromeus* had no defences other than their speed. Their young may have needed to be strong runners from the moment they hatched in order to escape predators and survive to adulthood. The hatchlings of larger plant-eating dinosaurs could have relied more upon the size and strength of their parents to protect them during their early weeks of helplessness.

Duckbills such as *Hypacrosaurus* (see page 33) might still have needed to grow quickly in order to join the annual migration. With the first change of season after the young hatched, the duckbills might have moved to new feeding grounds. In order to be big enough to migrate with the adults, the youngsters would have needed to grow fast. However, the rate of growth for these dinosaurs is not yet known.

# CENTROSAUR CATASTROPHE

Remains of thirty-seven different species of dinosaurs are preserved in the badland rocks of Dinosaur Provincial Park in Alberta, Canada. At least fifteen of these species are preserved in dozens of whole skeletons. A bed of hundreds of broken bones from many centrosaurs allows scientists to tell how a herd of these horned dinosaurs met their end 75 million years ago.

## THE END OF A HERD

**A herd of horned dinosaurs**, young and old, attempts to cross a river in search of fresh feeding grounds. There are more than 300 individuals in the herd.

Like many dinosaurs, these animals can probably swim well. But, after recent rains, the current is too fast and the water too high for the dinosaurs to swim to the opposite bank. As they enter the water, they panic and thrash wildly, trampling one another and breaking many of their limbs (1). These unfortunate animals drown. Their bodies are washed up on the riverbanks by the powerful waters.

A bed of centrosaur dinosaur bones appears to be just a jumble of broken bones. To the trained eye of a palaeontologist, however, stories of death and life are suggested by these fossils. The many sizes of limb bones indicate that the herd included animals of many ages. The sandstone and the pattern of how the bones were piled show that the animals' bones were jumbled by a fast-flowing stream. Then they were preserved by a blanket of river-bottom sand that later turned to stone. But how do scientists know that the animals broke one another's bones in a stampede? They don't.

Scientists think these dinosaurs died in an unusual situation because of the way the bones are broken. The fractures are spiral in shape. These 'greenstick' breaks look like the uneven and incomplete break made when a green twig is bent or twisted. These fractures show that the bones were broken before they became fossils, probably within two years before death.

The bloated bodies of drowned dinosaurs lie on the riverbank. *Albertosaurus* are attracted by the smell of the rotting flesh **(2)**. They gnaw and strip the bones clean.

Over years, the river waters rise slowly and steadily. The water washes over the bones and moves them slightly **(3)**. The river carries sand and silt downstream, which settles over the bones. Over thousands of years it packs down. Minerals enter into the bones, making them harden into fossils. Millions of years later scientists uncover the bones for us to see **(4)**.

PLATEOSAURUS        PARASAUROLOPHUS        TYRANNOSAURUS REX        TROODON

Instead of a stampede, these centrosaurs might have died in a drought. As the herd searched for food and water, they became weaker and sicker. Near death, they collapsed one by one, trampling the weakest and the first to die before the last of them collapsed.

Other marks on the bones and cleaner breaks show that after these animals died they were eaten by predators. The marks match the teeth of large predators such as *Albertosaurus*.

## BRAINY DINOSAURS

The illustration above show different dinosaurs with their heads drawn the same size. The bony braincase that cups the brain may be fossilized. Brain weights compared to total body weights give rough measurements of the relative intelligence of dinosaurs. The meat-eater *Troodon* weighed 50 kilos and had a brain of 45 grams, yet it was probably the most intelligent of all dinosaurs. The human brain weighs about 1.4 kilos. A duckbill, *Parasaurolophus*, had a 0.3-kilo brain. The largest dinosaur brain – from a 7-tonne *Tyrannosaurus* – weighed 0.5 kilos.

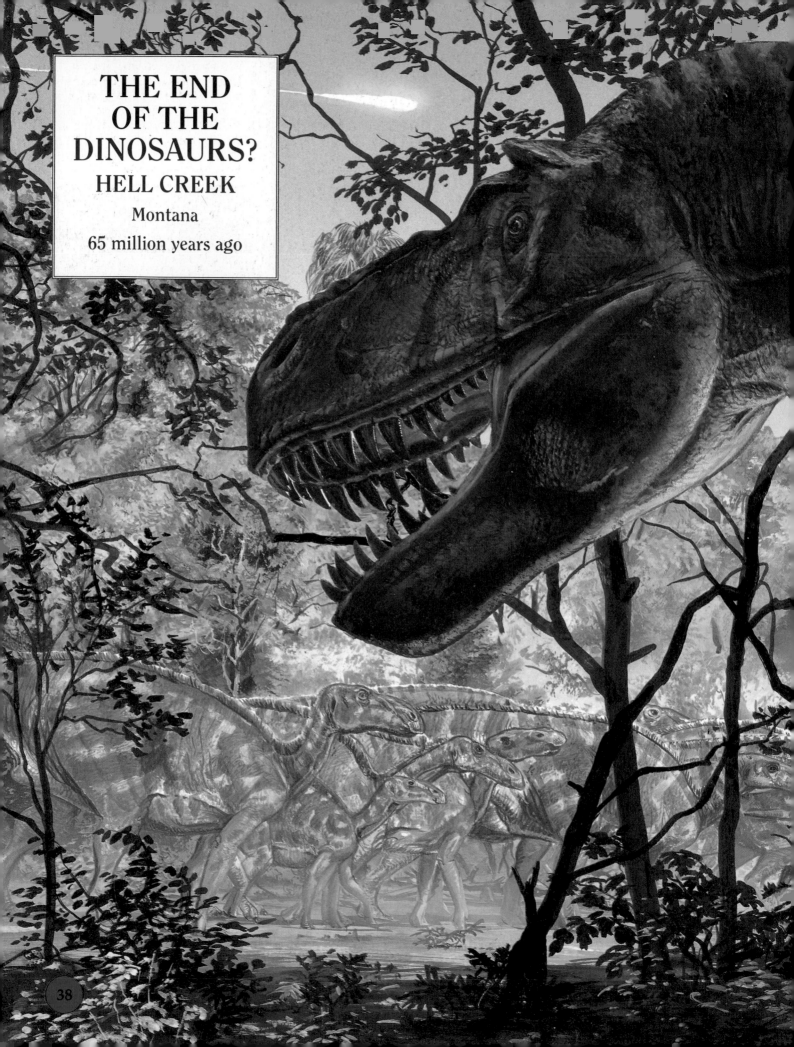

# THE END OF THE DINOSAURS?

## HELL CREEK

Montana

65 million years ago

Hidden among the trees of a forest, a *Tyrannosaurus rex* eyes a herd of duckbills, deciding which animal might become its next meal. A dragonfly flutters around the *T. rex* as a heavily armoured dinosaur looks on from a distance. An asteroid shoots across the sky.

# END OF THE LINE

The lush world of 65 million years ago contained the last communities of dinosaurs ever to walk the Earth. They included the best plant-chewers and some of the smartest, fastest and most powerful meat-eating dinosaurs ever. Yet, within a million years dinosaurs were extinct.

What killed the dinosaurs? Scientists are not certain. One of the most popular recent theories is that a huge asteroid crashed into the Earth. The enormous collision would have sent a cloud of dust into the atmosphere, blocking the sunlight. Fires from the explosion would have added to the dust cloud and the heat. Shifting temperatures could have killed many animals and plants, including dinosaurs and giant reptiles of the sea and air.

Whether the end of the dinosaurs was caused by an asteroid impact, volcanic eruption or slow change in climate and sea levels remains a mystery. There have been a handful of mass extinctions in the history of life. One of the most serious struck 65 million years ago. In the 163 million year history of dinosaurs, the world of the very last dinosaurs is the one we know best, but it is still largely a mystery.

Many fossils of these dinosaurs have been found in eastern Montana at a dig site known as Hell Creek. A range of herbivores and carnivores has been found, including fossils of the most famous of all dinosaurs, *Tyrannosaurus rex*.

**Following the impact of a giant asteroid,** the sun is coloured red, since much of its warming light is blocked by dust in the air. The land can no longer support dinosaurs. Small mouse- and opossum-like mammals scurry over the corpse of a dead and decaying *Tyrannosaurus*. They clamber, too, on the dead branches of a nearby tree.

**Hell Creek – Today** In a remote stretch of badlands in eastern Montana, sandstone cliffs and valleys expose rocks from 65 million years ago – the end of the Cretaceous Period and the beginning of the following Tertiary Period. Much of the land is used for grazing cattle. Here palaeontologists are using a mechanical shovel to raise a huge slab of rock containing fossils and load it on to a lorry.

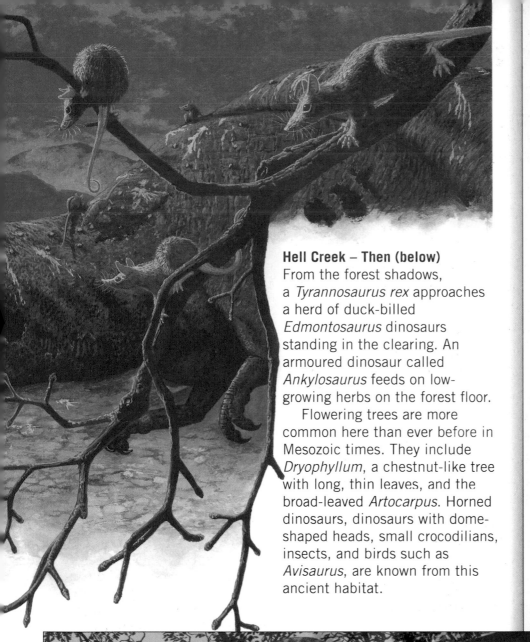

**Hell Creek – Then (below)**
From the forest shadows, a *Tyrannosaurus rex* approaches a herd of duck-billed *Edmontosaurus* dinosaurs standing in the clearing. An armoured dinosaur called *Ankylosaurus* feeds on low-growing herbs on the forest floor.

Flowering trees are more common here than ever before in Mesozoic times. They include *Dryophyllum*, a chestnut-like tree with long, thin leaves, and the broad-leaved *Artocarpus*. Horned dinosaurs, dinosaurs with dome-shaped heads, small crocodilians, insects, and birds such as *Avisaurus*, are known from this ancient habitat.

# FACT FILE

**Montana, Then and Now**
The Montana of today is far different from the same land 65 million years ago. By the end of the age of dinosaurs, the continents had almost reached their current positions. But the world was still much warmer and there were no polar ice caps.

Globe shows the position of the continents now.

**ANIMALS**
1. *Ankylosaurus* (ANK-ee-lo-SAW-rus)
2. Dragonfly
3. *Edmontosaurus* (ed-MON-toe-SAW-rus)
4. *Tyrannosaurus rex* (ti-RAN-o-SAW-rus REX)

**PLANTS**
5. *Dryophyllum* trees (DRY-o-FILL-um)
6. Herbs

ALSO AT THIS SITE:
*Avisaurus* (AY-vi-SAW-rus)
Crocodilians
Flowering trees
*Metasequoia* (MET-a-si-KOY-ah) conifers

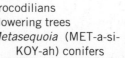

41

# TOOTHED TYRANT

Like the other tyrannosaurs that appeared in the last 10 million years of the dinosaurs' existence, *Tyrannosaurus rex* had particularly large, strong jaws and teeth. But was *T. rex* really a killer most of the time? Or did it mostly scavenge for food? Palaeontologists have differing opinions about *T. rex*'s feeding behaviour.

**T. rex had a deep and heavy skull.** A hinged lower jaw helped it open its mouth wide.

**Skull of T. rex** shows thick pointed teeth and a wide band of muscle that moved the hinged jaws.

*TYRANNOSAURUS REX*

## TYRANNOSAURUS REX
**Meaning of name:** 'Tyrant lizard king'
**Order:** Saurischia
**Size, Weight:** 12 metres long, 7 tonnes or more
**Location:** Western North America
**Diet:** Meat

*Tyrannosaurus*'s front limbs were so tiny that they could not touch each other. Yet they were strong, able to lift more than 200 kilos. However, its killing weapons – powerful muscular jaws – were enormous. More than 1.5 metres long, its skull held about fifty teeth the size of bananas. Each tooth was thick and pointed, good for breaking through bones. The jagged edges of these teeth could slice like a steak knife through thick muscle (see also pages 6–7).

### Scavenger or predator?
*Tyrannosaurus rex* was a huge meat-eater. Instead of hunting (below right), it might have fed off the carcasses of dead animals when they were available (below left). Huge herds of horned dinosaurs like *Triceratops* may have provided carrion.

# PLANTS

*Erlangdorfia* was a flowering tree. Sixty-five million years ago, it grew 15 metres tall in the Hell Creek area. Its trunk was 30 centimetres or more in diameter, and its leaves had two or three lobes. Plant fossils from Hell Creek show that by this time, more than nine in every ten plants were flowering plants and trees, not conifers or ferns.

## INSECTS

The earliest bees and ants in the fossil record were found in amber from 65 million years ago. Slightly older plant fossils from Wyoming show damage from insects, including moths. Moth larvae had mined their way through the leaves of a tree.

## *AVISAURUS*

**Meaning of name:** 'Bird reptile'
**Order:** Enantiornithiformes
**Size, Weight:** 60- to 120- centimetre wingspan, about 1 kilo
**Location:** Montana
**Diet:** Meat

*Avisaurus* was a hawk-sized bird that probably fed on small animals, as many small birds do today. So far, it is known only from its foot and leg bones. *Avisaurus* belongs to an extinct family not closely related to modern birds.

AVISAURUS

## *ANKYLOSAURUS*

**Meaning of name:** 'Fused lizard'
**Order:** Ornithischia
**Size, Weight:** 6 metres, 3 to 4 tonnes
**Location:** Montana and Alberta
**Diet:** Plants

*Ankylosaurus* was one of the last and largest of the club-tailed armoured dinosaurs. Built low to the ground, it had armour over much of its body, including its

eyelids. Its tail club, which was made of several armour plates and was swung by the animal's stiff tail, may have been a good weapon. Barnum Brown of the American Museum of Natural History discovered *Ankylosaurus* nearly a century ago.

Although *Ankylosaurus* has been famous for nearly 100 years, only three good specimens, none complete, have ever been found. It is named after the many fused bones in its skeleton. With its horny beak, it was highly adapted to crop and chew plants.

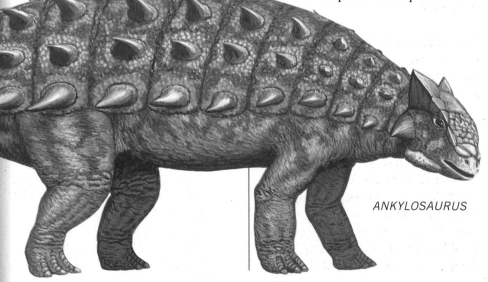

ANKYLOSAURUS

43

# ACCIDENTAL DEATH?

For decades scientists have debated the question 'What killed the dinosaurs?'. Some of them have argued that dinosaurs died of digestion problems, or disease, or climate change. The cause remains unknown, but some interesting evidence in the last two decades supports another theory: a disaster from outer space.

The habitat of what is now Hell Creek Formation in Montana underwent a dramatic change 65 million years ago. Changes in leaf fossils show the effects of sudden cold and drier weather. In Montana and around the world, many plants and animals disappeared. An asteroid blasted a huge crater off the coast of Mexico at this time. The collision may have triggered fires and volcanic eruptions around the world. Huge clouds of dust thrown into the atmosphere first warmed the Earth, then cooled it to temperatures too low for dinosaurs and some other animals. For many creatures, the result was extinction.

1

2

3

4

**An asteroid is pulled towards the Earth** by the powerful force of gravity. Going through the atmosphere, friction turns the asteroid red hot. Much of it burns away, but it is still nearly 10 kilometres wide when it hits **(1)**.

The fiery blast makes a crater nearly 200 kilometres wide and sets off volcanoes round the world. As duck-billed dinosaurs browse, a volcano erupts **(2)**, destroying vegetation and killing many animals in the area.

Dust from fires, volcanic eruptions and the asteroid impact cut off much of the light **(3)** needed by many plants and animals to survive. Smoke fills the air. Shock waves from the impact create floods from huge sea waves.

The land grows cooler and darker **(4)**. Rainfall is highly acid. Many kinds of plants die, leading to the deaths of plant-eating dinosaurs. Eventually, the various meat-eating dinosaurs have no plant-eaters to consume. They also die.

So what actually killed off the last dinosaurs? Some scientists have suggested that the smoke and ash from the asteroid impact 65 million years ago first heated and then cooled the atmosphere. This killed off plant life, dinosaurs and several other forms of large animals. Other scientists suggest that volcanic eruptions produced the same weather changes. Acid rain, cancer-causing radiation from the impact of objects from space, diseases, and gradual climate change are other proposed dinosaur-killers.

**Mass extinctions**
Dates are in millions of years ago.

TRIASSIC
250
225
JURASSIC
200
175
150
CRETACEOUS
125
100
65

Extinction of the dinosaurs

Peaks are about every 26 million years. The higher the peak, the more species died out.

Orange shaded area represents numbers of species of animals and plants becoming extinct. Peaks represent mass extinctions. Green, yellow and blue bands are geological periods.

**Trees are felled by a natural disaster (above).** In human history there has never been an asteroid impact in an area where many people live. A possible collision of an asteroid with the Earth took place in Siberia in 1908. It caused fires and flattened trees for many kilometres around.

Scientists imagine that the effect of an asteroid striking the Earth would be much like the devastation of a nuclear war. When an atomic bomb is set off, it creates a huge mushroom-shaped cloud that sends smoke and dust high into the air. The air is heated to a burning temperature for kilometres around. The only two atomic bombs set off in populated areas, in Japan during World War II, had terrible effects on all local life.

**Some scientists have detected a pattern** in the timing of the extinction events that strike the Earth. They see them occurring every 26 million years. The extinctions may be related to the cycle of the approach of some comets to the Earth. Impacts of some of these objects with the Earth at these times may cause the extinctions. Scientists who study fossils now think that changes in life-forms may not proceed at a steady pace. Brief periods of drastic change, including major extinctions, shape the history of life. So dinosaurs may have started their rise and met their end through accidental tragedies.

# EADING THE OCKS

The rocks and fossils of the Hell Creek Formation offer some of the best clues about the world of the last dinosaurs and the start of the Age of Mammals. From fossils of animals and plants, and from rare minerals in the rocks, scientists find clues to the life and death of the last dinosaurs. Many scientists do think that birds are living dinosaurs, direct descendants of meat-eating dinosaurs.

Scientists examine **Tyrannosaurus rex fossil bones** embedded in rock at Hell Creek Formation. At Hell Creek there are distinct layers of sandstone and coal. A layer of black coal marks the end of the Age of Dinosaurs. A few centimetres below that, scientists have discovered high concentrations of the rare element iridium. It is likely that the iridium came from a meteorite striking the Earth.

The most complete *T. rex* skeleton was found in the neighbouring state of South Dakota in 1990. It was discovered by prospector Sue Hendrickson and has been nicknamed 'Sue'.

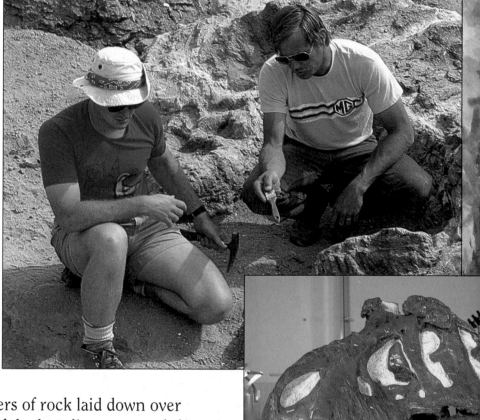

In the Hell Creek Formation, layers of rock laid down over millions of years contain fossils of the last dinosaurs and the animals and plants that lived with them. Above these layers are rocks formed in the hundreds of thousands of years after the dinosaurs disappeared. Near the boundary between the Age of Dinosaurs and the Age of Mammals, scientists discovered a layer of rock that is rich in iridium. Iridium is a rare element on Earth. It is more common in rocks, such as meteorites, which come from outer space. At several other places on the Earth, similar bands of iridium-rich clay have been detected from the same period. Other scientists point to changes in the shapes of leaf fossils at this time. These changes seem to reflect adaptation to a drastic change in climate as the Earth underwent a period of cooler temperatures.

**The skull of a *Tyrannosaurus rex*** exhibited at the American Museum of Natural History in New York. The skull is mostly original bone, not a cast. A new complete reconstruction of *T. rex* now stands in the museum.

The extinction of the dinosaurs left a gap in the web of life for large animals to fill. Mammals evolved into many new types of larger sizes and filled this gap. Now most of the common large creatures on land are mammals. Sixty-four million years after dinosaurs died out, humans evolved. Some day, in the distant future, humans and other mammals may become extinct as well. New creatures will rule the Earth. Dinosaurs will never live again, but their descendants, birds, live on.

**A *Tyrannosaurus rex* rampages** through the forest 65 million years ago. A tiny mammal watches, safely hidden on a tree branch. The mammal will survive the great extinction that is about to wipe out many species. Why? Perhaps mammals' small size or modest food needs helped them survive.

**An animated model** of the head and shoulders of a *Tyrannosaurus rex.*

# INDEX